Bible Stories for

Early Readers

God Adds Oil

Lavaun Linde
Mary Quishenberry

Some New Words

that, grave, Elisha,
cash slave, what,
oil, all, back, you, thank

Alpha Omega Publications®

804 N. 2nd Ave. E., Rock Rapids, IA 51246-1759

Bible Stories for . . . .

Early Readers

God Adds Oil

The Widow's Oil
2 Kings 4:1–7

By Lavaun Linde
   Mary Quishenberry
Illustrated by
   Joe Maniscalco

1

"Lads, it is sad that Dad is in the grave, but God will take care of us. God will help us take care of that big bill, too. Lads, let us go and see Elisha, the man of God."

3

"Sir, help us. Dad has left us with this big bill and no cash.

4

And if we can not take
care of this bill a man
will take the lads and
make them slaves."

"Ma'am, what is at
home?"

"H'mm.
Sir, just a jug of oil."

"Go to lots of homes,"
Elisha tells Mom, "and
get jugs and pots, not
just 1—
not just 2—
but get lots and lots of
jugs and pots."

"Take them home. Tip the jug of oil and fill all the jugs and the pots to the top."

The lads get jugs and pots.

13

The lads get more and
more till the home has
lots and lots of jugs
and pots.

Mom gets the jug of oil.

As Mom tips the jug,
God adds more and
more oil.

God adds oil to fill all the jugs and the pots to the top.

Mom runs back to the man of God. "Sir, the lads got lots and lots of jugs and pots. And God gave us the oil to fill all those jugs and pots to the top."

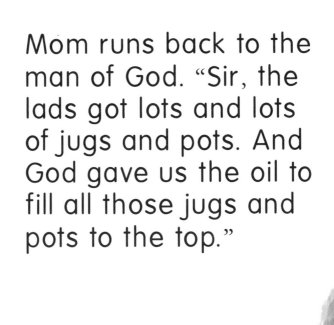

24

"Go and sell the oil,
then take care of that
bill," Elisha tells Mom.
"And with the cash that
is left, take care
of the lads
and you."

25

Mom sells the oil.

Mom takes care of the big bill and runs on home.

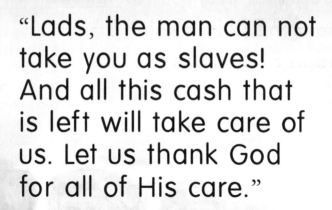

"Lads, the man can not
take you as slaves!
And all this cash that
is left will take care of
us. Let us thank God
for all of His care."

God has a promise for me in
Psalm 55:22, Psalm 34:7,
and in Philippians 4:19.

Something to Think About

1. After Mom sold the oil, what did she do with all the money?

2. Mom's one pot of oil filled many jugs and pots. How did Mom feel about so much oil coming from her one pot?

3. What can I do when I need help?

A Progressive Word Building Series

Bible Stories for . . . .

Early Readers

Children
Parents
and
Teachers
LOVE them

LR0201-Aug '07 Printing

ISBN 978-0-7403-0116-2

9 780740 301162

Bible Stories for . . . .

Early Readers

Zacchaeus'
Cash Bag

Lavaun Linde
Mary Quishenberry

Some New Words

Zacchaeus, from, stole,
come, short, tree,
under, forgave

Alpha Omega Publications®

804 N. 2nd Ave. E., Rock Rapids, IA 51246-1759

Bible Stories for . . . .

Early Readers

Zacchaeus' Cash Bag

Luke 19: 1-9

By Lavaun Linde
Mary Quishenberry
Illustrated by
Joe Maniscalco

Zacchaeus has a job.
His job is to get the tax
from the moms and the
dads. Zacchaeus puts the
tax in a box.

Zacchaeus has a bag.
Zacchaeus takes more
cash than the tax. He
hides this cash in his bag.

A man tells Zacchaeus, "Jesus likes the tax men, but Jesus tells the tax men to take just the tax and no more cash than that."

"I am sad I did not take just the tax. I am sad I stole the cash from all those moms and dads."

Zacchaeus runs home
and gets his cash bags.

"I will take back all the
cash that I stole. And I
will add lots more cash
to it."

Zacchaeus takes the cash to lots of moms and dads.

"Sir, I am sad I stole the cash from you. Here is 4 times more cash than I stole."

"I am so glad that I gave back all that cash."

17

"Jesus is here! Jesus is here!" a man yells. "Jesus will come up the lane."

"I must go and see Jesus." Zacchaeus runs to see Him.

"I see lots of kids and moms and dads but I can not see Jesus! I am just too short!"

"A tree!!
I will get up
in that big tree
then I can see!"

23

Zaccheus gets up in the big tree. "Ahhh, at last I can see Jesus."

Jesus walks up the lane
and stops under the tree.

"Zacchaeus come. I will
go home with you."

"Jesus will go home with me! He must love me! I love Him!"

"Jesus, here I come!"

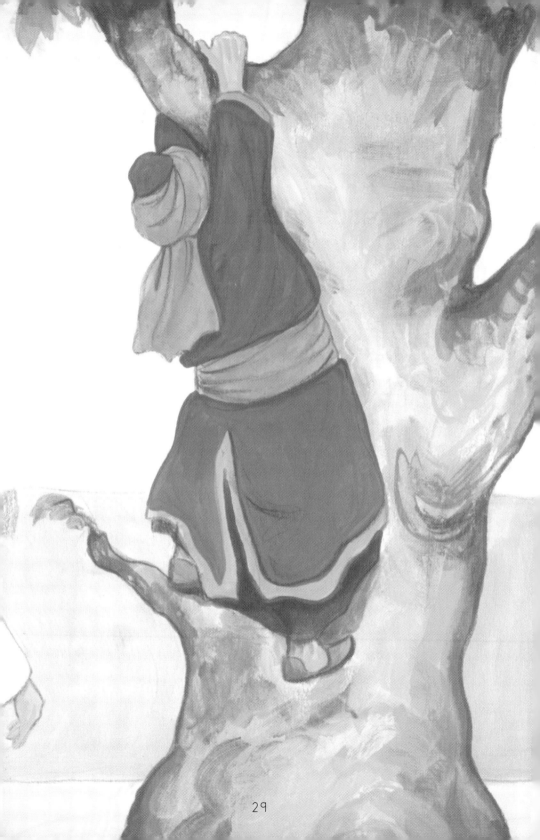

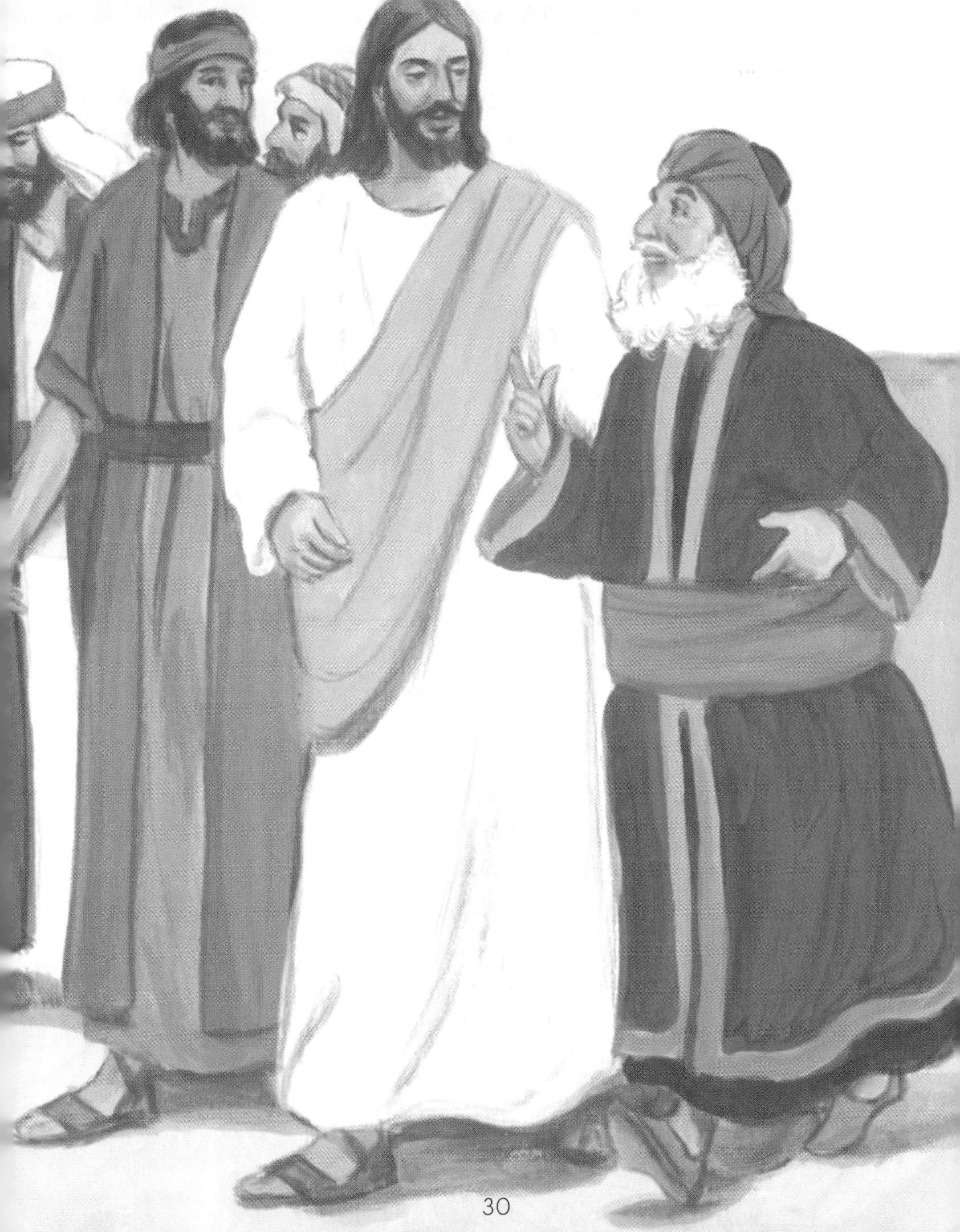

"Jesus, I am so glad you will go home with me and that You forgave me."

God has a promise for me in 1 John 1:9.

Something to Think About

1. What was Zacchaeus' job?

2. How did it make Zacchaeus feel to give back lots more cash than he stole?

3. If I have taken things that do not belong to me, what should I do?

A Progressive Word Building Series

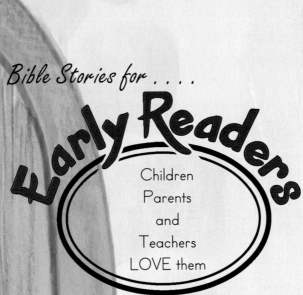

Bible Stories for . . . .

Early Readers

Children
Parents
and
Teachers
LOVE them

LR0202-Aug '07 Printing

ISBN 978-0-7403-0117-9

9 780740 301179

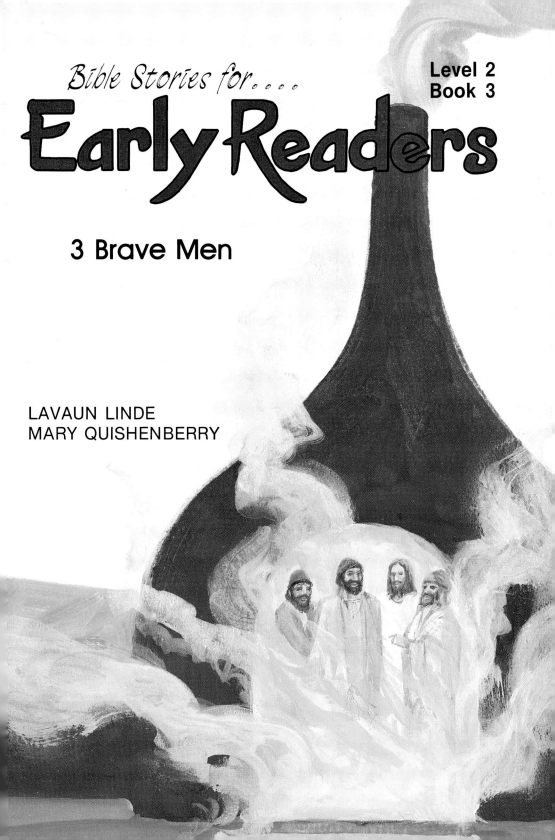

Some New Words
do, be, when, begins,

bow, down, three,

true, quick, now,

flame, jumps, Son, trust

Bradshaw Publishers
P.O. Box 277
Bryn Mawr, CA 92318

ISBN 0-945107-07-2

Early Readers

3 Brave Men

Shadrach, Meshach, and Abednego
Daniel 3:1-28

By Lavaun Linde
    Mary Quishenberry
Illustrated by
    Joe Maniscalco

The king has
a big fake god made.

The king tells his men,
"Go to the top men
in all the land.
Tell them to come
and see the god!"

The king's men rush
to do the job.

"Men, come and see
the king's god
on this date!
Do not be late!"

The time comes.
The king's top men
from all the land
race to the place
and face the fake god.

"When the tune begins,
you must all bow down
to this god."
the king tells them.

The tune begins,
but three men
do not bow down
to the fake god.

The three men love the true God and dare to be brave.

The king's men see
all the men bow down—
but the three.
"What!
Those three men
do not bow!"

"Quick! Let us run
and tell the king!"

"O King,
three men did not bow!"

The mad king yells,
"Go
and get them
for me!"

"Is it true that you three men
did not bow down
to the god that I had made?

When the tune begins this time,
if you do not bow down,
I will put you in that fire!"
the king yells.
"And what god
can save you
then."

The three men
still dare to be brave.
"O King, the true God
can save us from the fire
and from you.
We will not bow down
to the fake god."

"Men, make the fire
7 times as hot as it is now,"
the king yells.

The men do the job.

Then the king's men
put lots of rope
on the three men
and toss them into the fire!

The three men do not get hot
but the ropes go up in flames.
The men get up
and walk in the fire.

The king gets pale!
He jumps up!
"What do I see?

We put three men in the fire.
But I—I—I—see—
I see 4 men,
and the last man
is like the Son of God."

"Come here!"
the king yells
to the three men.

All see
the three brave men
walk from the fire.

The king's top men
go back home
and tell of the true God
and of the three brave men
that trust in Him.

God has a promise for me
in Hebrews 13:5, 6
and in Psalm 56:11.

Something to Think About

1. Who was in the fire
   with Shadrach, Meshach,
   and Abednego?

2. How did the king feel
   when he saw 4 men
   walking in the fire?

3. When people ask me
   to do things
   that I know are wrong,
   what should I do?

A Progressive Word Building Series

Level 1

Book 1	**Not a Bed**	Baby Jesus
Book 2	**I Will Help**	The Good Samaritan
Book 3	**Mom and the Lad**	Elijah and the Widow of Zarephath
Book 4	**The Lad's Bag**	The Five Loaves and Two Fish
Book 5	**Daniel and the Big Cats**	Daniel in the Lions' Den

Level 2

Book 1	**God Adds Oil**	The Widow's Oil
Book 2	**Zacchaeus' Cash Bag**	
Book 3	**3 Brave Men**	Shadrach, Meshach, and Abednego
Book 4	**7 Dips**	Naaman Finds a Cure
Book 5	**Jonah's Ride**	

Level 3

Book 1	**The Ten Lepers**	
Book 2	**Pigs, You Stink**	The Prodigal Son
Book 3	**The Big Quake**	Paul and Silas
Book 4	**Joseph and His Coat**	
Book 5	**The Dreams Come True**	Joseph as Ruler in Egypt

LITHO U.S.A. CP40472

Bible Stories for

Early Readers

Children
Parents
and
Teachers
LOVE them

ISBN 0-945107-07-2

Bible Stories for . . . .

Level 2
Book 4

Early Readers

7 Dips

Lavaun Linde
Mary Quishenberry

Some New Words

Naaman, girl, white,
himself, helper,
river, are

Alpha Omega Publications®

804 N. 2nd Ave. E., Rock Rapids, IA 51246-1759

Bible Stories for . . . . .

Early Readers

7 Dips

Naaman Finds a Cure
2 Kings 5:1–16

By Lavaun Linde
   Mary Quishenberry
Illustrated by
   Joe Maniscalco

"I am a slave in a land miles and miles from Mom and Dad. I can not go home, but God will take care of me."

4

"It is a big job to take care of Naaman and his wife's home," the girl prays to God. "Help me with this job. And help Naaman and his wife to love You."

6

Naaman's wife tells the girl, "Naaman has white spots on him. He is sick. I am sad."

"The man of God can make Naaman well," the girl tells Naaman's wife.

Naaman and his men go
to see the man of God.
Naaman tells himself,
"The man of God will see
me and make me well."

10

But the man of God sends
his helper to see Naaman.
The helper tells Naaman,
"Go to the river.
Dip in it 7 times,
and God will
make you well."

"What! the man of God will not take the time to see me and make me well!" Naaman tells his men. "And what is more, I am to go and dip in that river. I will not go!"

13

"Let us go to the river."

No! It has mud. It is not fit for a dip."

"Come on so you can get well!"

16

At last Naaman tells his men, "I-will-go."

17

Naaman dips in the river 1
time. He still has the spots.

2 times. He has spots.
Naaman dips 3, 4, 5, 6
times and he still has the
spots.

"Just one more dip in the river!" Naaman makes his last dip. "I am well! I am well!" Naaman yells.

Naaman rides back to see the man of God. "Thank you! Thank you!" Naaman tells him.

"Now men, let us go home." Naaman and his men rush home.

"I am well!" Naaman yells
to his wife and the girl.

"The girl's God made me well!" Naaman tells his wife. Naaman and his wife are so glad! "No more fake gods for us!"

The girl prays to God, "I love you and I am glad that You made Naaman well. I am so glad Naaman and his wife love You now! Thank You, God."

God has a promise for me in James 5:15.

Something to Think About

1. The slave girl had to work day after day. Who did she ask to help her?

2. How did Naaman and his wife feel about having a slave girl that loved the true God?

3. What can I do to be a missionary like the slave girl?

A Progressive Word Building Series

Level 1
Book 1 Not a Bed
        Baby Jesus

Book 2 I Will Help
        The Good Samaritan

Book 3 Mom and the Lad
        Elijah and the Widow of Zarephath

Book 4 The Lad's Bag
        The Five Loaves and Two Fish

Book 5 Daniel and the Big Cats
        Daniel in the Lions' Den

Level 2
Book 1 God Adds Oil
        The Widow's Oil

Book 2 Zacchaeus' Cash Bag

Book 3 3 Brave Men
        Shadrach, Meshach and Abednego

Book 4 7 Dips
        Naaman Finds a Cure

Book 5 Jonah's Ride

Level 3
Book 1 The Ten Lepers

Book 2 Pigs, You Stink
        The Prodigal Son

Book 3 The Big Quake
        Paul and Silas

Book 4 Joseph and His Coat

Book 5 The Dreams Come True
        Joseph as Ruler in Egypt

Bible Stories for . . . .

Early Readers

Children
Parents
and
Teachers
LOVE them

LR0204 - Sep '08 Printing

ISBN 978-0-7403-0119-3

9 780740 301193

Bible Stories for....

Early Readers

Jonah's Ride

LAVAUN LINDE
MARY QUISHENBERRY

Some New Words
have, want, Jonah,
boat, feel, sea, seek,
sleep, your, my, keep,
in side, sea weed, day, way

Bradshaw Publishers
P.O. Box 277
Bryn Mawr, CA 92318

ISBN 0-945107-09-9

Bible Stories for....

Early Readers

Jonah's Ride

Jonah 1-3

By Lavaun Linde
Mary Quishenberry
Illustrated by
Joe Maniscalco

"I have a place
I want you to go,"
God tells Jonah.
"It is full of men with sin.
Go and help them to love Me."

"I do not want
to do that job."
Jonah runs
and gets on a boat.
"I will get in this spot
to ride and hide
from God."
But Jonah
can not hide
from God.

All goes well,
till God sends a bad wind.
The boat tips from side to side,
as the waves rise and rise!!
The men in the boat
do not feel safe!!

The men bow down
to fake gods and beg,
"Help us now!"
But the boat still tips
from side to side
as the waves rise and rise.
The men see
that the fake gods
are of no help.

"What can we do now?"

The men toss lots and lots
in to the sea,
but the men
do not feel safe yet.

The man that runs the boat
yells to Jonah,
"Wake up!
This is no time to sleep!
Get up and ask your God
to save us!"

Jonah gets up.

Jonah tells the men on the boat,
"I am the blame for the bad wind
and the big waves.
Toss me in to the sea
and my God will stop the wind
and the waves."

The men
toss Jonah
into the sea.

God stops
the bad wind
and
the big waves.

The men in the boat pray
to Jonah's God,
"Thank You, God.
Thank You."

God loves Jonah
and sends a BIG FISH
to keep Jonah safe
in the sea.

Jonah rides and prays
the rest of the day.

"God, save me!
I do not like
to ride inside this fish!"
Jonah rides and prays
all the next day.

"God, I love You!
I do not want
to ride and hide this way."
Jonah rides and prays
for three days.

"God, You can save me.
Can I do that job?"
Jonah sobs.

God makes the BIG FISH
spit up Jonah onto the shore.

God tells Jonah,
"I love you,
and I still have the job
in that place
for you to do."

Jonah is glad
to do the job for God.
And best of all,
all the men in that place
get rid of sin.

God has a promise
for me in Joshua 1:9.

Something to Think About

1. Why did Jonah get on the boat?

2. How did Jonah feel
   about being
   inside the BIG FISH?

3. What kind of job does
   God have for me to do?

A Progressive Word Building Series

Level 1

Book 1   **Not a Bed**
Baby Jesus

Book 2   **I Will Help**
The Good Samaritan

Book 3   **Mom and the Lad**
Elijah and the Widow of Zarephath

Book 4   **The Lad's Bag**
The Five Loaves and Two Fish

Book 5   **Daniel and the Big Cats**
Daniel in the Lions' Den

Level 2

Book 1   **God Adds Oil**
The Widow's Oil

Book 2   **Zacchaeus' Cash Bag**

Book 3   **3 Brave Men**
Shadrach, Meshach, and Abednego

Book 4   **7 Dips**
Naaman Finds a Cure

Book 5   **Jonah's Ride**

Level 3

Book 1   **The Ten Lepers**

Book 2   **Pigs, You Stink**
The Prodigal Son

Book 3   **The Big Quake**
Paul and Silas

Book 4   **Joseph and His Coat**

Book 5   **The Dreams Come True**
Joseph as Ruler in Egypt

LITHO U.S.A. CP40492

Bible Stories for

Early Readers

Children
Parents
and
Teachers
LOVE them

ISBN 0-945107-09-9